WINNING THE DAY

Winning the Day

Gwynn Williams

BRYNTIRION PRESS

© Gwynn Williams 2002
First published, 2002
ISBN 1 85049 187 9

Cover design: J. Hurley Design Associates

Published by the Bryntirion Press
Bryntirion, Bridgend CF31 4DX, Wales, UK
Printed by Creative Print & Design, Ebbw Vale

Acknowledgements

The publishers are grateful to the Evangelical Fellowship of Congregational Churches for their encouragement and practical support in the production of this book.

They are also grateful to Kitty Lloyd Jones for her work in translating *Ennill Cymru i Grist,* the Welsh-language version published in 1999. This has been of considerable help in the preparation of the present volume, providing a basic structure for the incorporation of changes made when the addresses were subsequently delivered in English.

Foreword

The first time I saw Gwynn Williams was on a running track in Aberystwyth. He, I should hasten to add, was the athlete (he is still a fitness enthusiast) and I was the spectator. In fact he was training. Gwynn Williams was also busy training his mind: a Cambridge graduate in mathematics with a divinity degree from the University of Wales, at the time I met him he was engaged in researching the philosophy of religion.

Both the astuteness of Gwynn Williams' mind and the clarity of his thinking are apparent in these addresses, along with the pastoral awareness and missionary vision which come from years in the active local church ministry.

The addresses here were first given in English at the Millennium Family Conference of the Evangelical Fellowship of Congregational Churches held at Loughborough University in August 2000; they had previously been given in Welsh (and subsequently published in Welsh) at the Evangelical Movement of Wales Conference at Aberystwyth in 1998.

Gwynn Williams' theme is so important for our modern church life that the decision was taken to put the talks into print. It is not unfair to characterise much of our present-day evangelical Christianity as unthinking, materialistic and self-centred. Gwynn Williams' mind-set addresses confront such an attitude head on.

How are we to succeed as the Christian community in our contemporary society? Taking his cue from the past the author points us unmistakably and clearly to the present and the future. His message is important. You must read this book!

Alan Tovey
March 2002

Contents

Introduction

Now that we have crossed the threshold of the new millennium, we need to ask ourselves what task faces us as Christians in these islands. I feel sure that each one of us would wish to see the name of God magnified to a greater extent than in the past years, to see the trickle of conversions become a steady or even a swift-flowing stream, to see an increase in the number of churches that are spiritually alive, and all the people of this land glorifying God and worshipping the Lord Jesus Christ. But we know full well that what we long for will not come to pass unless the Holy Spirit be at work, and that is why many of us have faithfully prayed over many years that the promised Comforter may manifest his power in revival—that God may demonstrate that his arm is not shortened.

But as we pray for the Spirit, it is appropriate that we ask what else we should do, because as Christians we know that God would not have us sit idly by, waiting for something to happen. We need guidelines to direct our lives as individuals and as churches. What manner of people ought we to be as we pray for God's work in our land? Wherein lie our weaknesses, and what steps should we take to turn them into strengths? What are the tell-tale signs that we are slipping, and how can we reverse the trend? Where, precisely, do we fight the battle? Fighting the battles of the past will avail us nothing; times have changed. We no longer live in the thirties or the sixties of the twentieth century, but in the opening decade of the twenty-first. Where is today's battlefield? How are we to go about winning these islands once more to Christ?

The most successful period in the history of the Christian church was that of the first three centuries, when Christianity spread from the upper room in Jerusalem to the palace of the emperor in Rome. As we think of that wonderful period of success, we might well ask whether the early Christians have anything to teach us. What were the main features of the life of the church in the first three centuries? Certainly the Holy Spirit was at work, but what were the saints doing? Wherein lay their efforts, their emphases, in their personal lives and in the corporate life of the church?

One English historian who has made a study of the period has come to the conclusion that their success was due to the fact that 'they out-thought, they out-preached, they out-loved and out-suffered' their contemporaries.

As we face the current situation in our land, I cannot but feel that those four points are four issues that we, as evangelical Christians at the beginning of the twenty-first century, must contend with. That is, if we are to win the day for the Lord Jesus Christ, we must win the day in the realm of the mind, in the realm of proclaiming or preaching, in the realm of love—towards each other and the lost world outside—and, in doing so, we must be ready to suffer for the gospel and for the cause of Christ.

1
The realm of
the mind

Let us, in the first place, turn our attention to the battle to be won in the realm of the mind. As we shall see, this theme is of particular relevance to each one of us, and especially so to the younger generation—the generation that will be here for the next half-century.

On turning to the Scriptures, we find many an interesting exhortation in this context. We can do no better than begin with the two opening verses of Romans 12:

> Therefore, I urge you, brothers, in view of God's mercy, to offer your bodies as living sacrifices, holy and pleasing to God—this is your spiritual act of worship. Do not conform any longer to the pattern of this world, but be transformed by the renewing of your mind. Then you will be able to test and approve what God's will is—his good, pleasing and perfect will (Romans 12:1-2).

At this point there is a clear break in the epistle to the Romans. In the first eleven chapters Paul has been discussing doctrine: the first eight chapters explain the essence of Christianity, and the following three chapters deal with some doctrinal problems. And then in chapter 12 we have the significant word 'therefore'. Paul has dealt with the theology; he now gets down to the practicalities.

What ought to be true of you on the basis of what you believe? According to Paul, it is that you present your body as a living sacrifice, holy and pleasing to God. The 'reasonable service' (AV, NIV margin)—the very least that can be expected of Christians who have believed the first eleven chapters of Romans—is that they are now prepared to give all that they have to serve God.

The Christian mindset

How are they going to do that? In order to give all to God, says Paul, firstly, they must not be conformed to this world. There is a pagan, godless mindset from which Christians, on coming to this new life, must extricate themselves. That is the first step. At this juncture, a basic change must take place in the lives of Christian people: they must cease to conform to the world, or the society of which they are members, and must now discover, through the renewing of their minds, the Christian mindset.

How does this change come about? Well, says Paul, 'be transformed by the renewing of your mind'. In other words, Christians must refrain from pressing themselves into the mould of the world. Something radical must take place in their minds; their ways of thinking must be renewed, so that they might be able 'to test and approve what God's will is—his good, pleasing and perfect will'. It is impossible to live the Christian life as it ought to be lived unless the mind is first illumined and convinced. Therefore, the first thing that must happen is the renewing of the mind.

In his letter to the Ephesians Paul makes the same point, and he develops his argument in much the same way. First comes the doctrine, then he moves on to the practical application, telling us, in verse 22 of chapter 4, how we ought to live: 'You were taught, with regard to your former way of life, to put off your old self, which is being corrupted by its deceitful desires.' That is what you were before your conversion, that was the nature of your life, the nature of the 'old self'. But, says Paul, I want you to 'put on the new self, created to be like God in true righteousness and holiness'. That is the change he is looking for—the putting away of the old self and the putting on of the new.

What comes in the middle, between the two? Verse 23—'to be made new in the attitude of your minds'. If you are going to move from the old self to the new, something radical must happen in between. The mind must be convinced about the necessity of this change, or it will never come about.

Take particular notice of Paul's wording, 'to be made new in the *attitude* of your minds'. The mind, the brain, does not change when one is converted. Doubtless many young Christians, when studying for GCSEs, A levels or degree examinations, wish that were so! No, the mind does not change in any way; the ability and the attainment of the brain remain the same. It is the principle which controls the mind that changes. It is not that the Christian thinks about different things, but that he thinks about things differently. The Christian's whole way of thinking changes. The attitude of the mind is being renewed.

The apostle Peter comes to the same point in the first chapter of his first epistle. Again, the beginning of the epistle speaks about the Christian gospel, and then comes the practical application, when Peter tells us what kind of people we should be as saints:

Therefore, prepare your minds for action; be self-controlled; set your hope fully on the grace to be given you when Jesus Christ is revealed. As obedient children, do not conform to the evil desires you had when you lived in ignorance. But just as he who called you is holy, so be holy in all you do (verses 13-15).

What comes in between putting away the evil desires of the past and being self-controlled and obedient to Christ? '*Prepare your minds for action*'; or in the AV, 'Gird up the loins of your mind.' What we have here is a picture of a man running. As you know, long ankle-length clothes were worn in the Middle East, and any attempt to run a race thus dressed would be bound to end in a nasty tripping incident. To run successfully in a long garment, one must lift up the bottom section at least to above the knees— one must 'gird one's loins'. To put it in everyday language, Peter is saying that you must mentally roll up your sleeves or take off your coat. There needs to be an effort in the realm of the mind.

Who does the renewing of the mind? Here again we find the glorious balance of Scripture. In Ephesians 4:23 the verb 'to be made new' indicates that the renewing is something that happens to you—you are *to be renewed*. We can understand that, because it is the Holy Spirit who regenerates and renews our minds. But Peter in his epistle emphasises *our* contribution. He uses the imperative, 'prepare your minds for action': *we* are to do the work; it is to be *our* effort.

We must bring together what is said by both apostles. This renewing of the mind is not something that must be left completely to God; neither is it something that we must do in our own strength. It is a co-operation between God and man. As in the overall process of sanctification, where the Spirit sanctifies us but we are to work out our salvation in fear and trembling, so in the realm of the mind. The Spirit renews the mind, but we must co-operate, that we might develop a mature Christian mind. We are commanded to love God with all our heart, with all our strength, and with all our mind. Do we neglect this last aspect—to love God with our minds?

Why are there these exhortations at such crucial points in these epistles? The reason is that by the time the epistles were being written, the gospel had spread from the Jewish to the Gentile world. What was true of the Gentile world in New Testament times? Well, it was a pagan, pluralistic, superstitious and carnal world. In Colossians 1:21 Paul describes the believers before their conversion: 'Once you were alienated from God and were enemies in your minds because of your evil behaviour.' That is, their mindset, their thought processes, were different before their conversion. The carnal, superstitious pagan who worshipped a multiplicity of deities had his own way of thinking. But now, Paul says to them, you have been converted, you have been renewed in your minds, your mindset is totally different.

In the words of the historian who describes the success of the early church in the first three centuries, 'they out-thought' their contemporaries. They won the world for Christ on the battlefield of the mind. They thought about their faith, about the implications of their faith. They could see the world's standpoints and argue victoriously against them. They convinced the unbelieving world that the greatest wisdom lay in Christianity.

Its relevance today

Why is this issue so relevant at the start of this new millennium? In the first place, it is because we live in an age that sets more store on feelings and experience than on the mind.

That was not the case at the beginning of the last century. The important thing then was reason; the mind and the reason ruled supreme. Indeed, the mere mention of experience and feelings might be considered a sign of weakness. The vital questions then were: Is this true? Is it scientific?

I well remember the adverts of the early 1950s. In order to promote sales, advertisers assured us that a product had been scientifically proved or scientifically tested. If something was said to be 'scientific', then the issue was well and truly settled. There was a rationality about it, a reason behind it; the mind had been applied to it. That was the attitude of the age. But, as we know, things have changed.

The feel-good factor
The media provide ample proof of this change. Years ago, when something momentous happened in the world, the question asked

17

was, What is your *opinion*? And to form an opinion one must, of necessity, think. Nowadays, the question asked is, How do you *feel*? How do you feel about recent developments in Israel, in Northern Ireland, in Afghanistan? Reporters no longer wish to know your thoughts; what they want is an expression of your feelings—whether you are sad or happy.

The effect of this trend on our vocabulary is plain for all to see—the phrase 'the feel-good factor' is constantly bandied about. Not '*Is* it good?' but 'Does it *feel* good?' If it feels good, it *is* good, despite the fact that it may be indisputably evil! Something is happening in our day and age: the mind is being put to one side, and feelings and experiences are becoming increasingly important.

The image and the soundbite
At the same time, communication has changed. Messages no longer come via the ear, but via the eye. When they come to the ear, it is the words that are important, and hearing those words causes one to think. But when the eye is addressed, the images are the important things, and one does not need to think. These images immediately affect one's emotions and feelings, and the mind is bypassed.

The same change of emphasis is to be found in the world of politics, where the photocall is of far greater importance than the speech. If the Prime Minister wishes to inform the nation that he is interested in education, what better than a photocall—a picture of him sitting in a classroom with happy children around him—to give us the feeling that he is pro-education? It is a lovely picture. There is no mention of policies.

Then, again, we live in a world of slogans. No one wants a long, well-reasoned speech; all that is needed is a short, pithy sentence that sounds good. Such is the age. The emphasis has shifted away from the argument and logical thinking.

Our churches

In such an age we have to return to thinking. But why is it so important that we think? For one thing, these changes in society can affect our churches.

In so many evangelical churches today the emphasis is on experiences rather than on reading the Word, and on the singing rather than on the preaching. Because what we *see* is becoming more important than what we hear, drama and mime and suchlike get centre stage. You ask someone, 'What was the morning worship like today?' and you are told, 'I enjoyed it.' Not many years ago the response would have been, 'I learned something' or 'I understood something' or 'My mind was exercised and I saw a glimpse of the glory of God.' There is a danger that we might be moving with the age.

There is also a danger that conversions may become more emotional than intellectual. It frequently happens that gospel meetings or 'missions' are superficial and charged with emotion, and people profess conversion when nothing much has happened in their minds. Because there has been no renewing of the mind, the old self has not been put aside, nor has the new self been put on. There has been an emotional experience, but no inner change; the mind has not been saved.

It is vitally important that we realise these things, that we observe what is happening in our society, that we recognise the warning signs and refuse to sideline the mind. The early Christians won the day because they were victorious in the realm of the mind. We must follow their example.

Christian morality

This issue is also important from the standpoint of Christian morality. During recent years we have all been taken aback by reports that some of the most highly respected leaders of the evangelical world have fallen into blatant sin. The past decade has seen the ethical standards of Christians, especially of young Christians, falling apace, and we are more and more aware of the deterioration in moral standards.

Is it not true to say that one reason for this deterioration is that there are people who have not been truly convinced in their minds of what is right and what is wrong? Our young people, for example, are not entirely convinced that sex before marriage, or drunkenness, is always wrong. Christians of an earlier generation were a hundred per cent convinced of these things. Their minds were completely won over, and this protected them and kept them from putting themselves in situations where the possibility of a fall could arise.

Life has changed, and the mind of the Christian is under attack from all sides. Our minds have been so sullied by the world's standards that the things we considered transgressions ten years ago now appear comparatively innocuous. And once there is wrong thinking, wrongdoing is but a small step away.

These days, the moral standards of so many people are being conditioned by soap operas, the tabloid press, public opinion, American chat shows and the like. Those who make these their daily diet find that their thinking can become corrupted, unless they are absolutely clear in their minds as to what the Christian ethic is.

How we live is therefore important. We need to think and see clearly what God expects of us. We need our minds to be convinced by the absolutes of God. In 2 Corinthians 11:3 Paul puts it like this: 'I am afraid that just as Eve was deceived by the serpent's cunning, your minds may somehow be led astray from your sincere and pure devotion to Christ.' No one commits a sin unless it has first of all possessed his mind. When the mind has fallen, the body soon follows. And so, in Ephesians, as we have seen, the renewing of the mind comes between the 'putting off' and the 'putting on'. The 'putting on' can only be done successfully if the mind is totally captivated. Therefore Paul wrote to the Corinthians, 'We demolish arguments and every pretension that sets itself up against the knowledge of God, and we take captive every thought to make it obedient to Christ' (2 Corinthians 10:5). We need to bring back the mind for the sake of moral standards.

Our view of gifts

The way we, as evangelical churches, appreciate the gifts that God has given us shows how prone we are to neglect the mind. Is it not true to say that we set more value on Christians who are musically gifted and have communication skills than on those who are able theologians, great thinkers and scholars?

Imagine two young Christians, both recently converted from the world, seeking membership in a church. The elder meets them and asks what gifts they possess. The first says, 'I can play the guitar.' 'Great!' says the elder. 'Just what we need for the youth group.' The second Christian replies, 'I have a first-class degree in Greek and Hebrew.' 'Oh! Interesting! But we don't know what we can do with you in our church.'

Our appreciation of gifts has changed. Gifts that have to do with the mind are no longer seen as important. Yes, it is true that God has given us diverse gifts, the musician's gift among them. But we need in the church the gifts of the theologian, the teacher and the scholar , for this is one way of ensuring the future.

Are we not greatly indebted to those who possessed gifts of the mind—scholars such as William Tyndale in England and William Morgan in Wales, who translated the Bible into the vernacular? Where would either country's Christianity be, were it not for their untiring efforts—in the case of the former, against great odds and bitter opposition? Should we not thank God that he gave them, his servants, not musical gifts but linguistic gifts in Greek and Hebrew—gifts of the mind? In his Prologue to the first printed English Bible, William Tyndale wrote:

For we have not received the gifts of God for ourselves only, or for to hide them; but for to bestow them unto the honouring of God and Christ and edifying of the congregation, which is the body of Christ.

We need the thinkers, we need the Greek and Hebrew scholars, we need the theologians. For we are not going to out-think the world if we do not have them.

A ghetto mentality

A further reason why giving priority to the mind is so relevant in our day is that it provides us with a weapon to contend with the world's arguments. The dumbing down of the mind means that we are not producing able thinkers, who can oppose the philosophy and concepts of a secular age. The early church had men who out-thought the pagans around them. This is what David Cook, who works in the world of medical problems and is familiar with medical ethics, says in his book, *Blind Alley Beliefs*:

> For too long Christians have had a ghetto mentality. Faced with the growth of science and humanism, we have retreated into individualism and hidden our gospel under a bushel . . . We must go out and take on the alternative worldviews, showing how they are inadequate, and that Christianity, truly understood and practised, is more than adequate for every need. The truth of the gospel far outweighs all other alternatives.

There may be a danger that our evangelical churches are retreating into an evangelical ghetto, unable to gainsay the arguments that are brought against them. It is about time we stood up and went into battle once again. Paul argued with the philosophers. He was going to out-think them, so that their thinking, presuppositions and lifestyle were challenged.

If we have the truth of God and the wisdom of God, why should we be afraid? We need to develop a distinctively Christian mind that will influence our world socially, culturally, and politically, and, most important, affect every aspect of our lives, particularly the moral and spiritual dimensions.

Developing the Christian mind

But how does one go about developing the Christian mind? What is the initial step on that road? The answer is simple: the Word of God must be allowed to take full authority over our minds, so that we think as Christians rather than as the world.

In Hebrews 10:16, God is quoted as saying, 'I will put my laws in their hearts, and I will write them on their minds.' That is the first step in the renewal of the mind: it must be imprinted with God's laws. Psalm 1, describing the godly man, tells us that 'his delight is in the law of the LORD, and on his law he meditates day and night'. The result is that he is one who is immovable, 'like a tree planted by streams of water'. He who has steeped himself in God's truths and submitted his whole way of thinking to their authority has a scriptural mindset: not the mind of the television programmers or the daily newspaper, but of the Word of God. This, according to Paul, is the way to know the good, pleasing and perfect will of God.

The whole of our thinking has to be subject at every turn to the whole content of the Bible. But, you say, this is an enormous task; the Bible is huge; how can I possibly keep it in my mind all of the time? How can I apply it to an argument or discussion or decision? The task is well-nigh impossible!

On one level that is true, but there is a way that will help us, namely, to gather the contents of the Bible under easy headings that we can remember. D. A. Carson in *The Gagging of God*, and in other books he has written, speaks of what he calls 'the Bible plot line'. He does this with reference to evangelism in a pagan world, arguing that we must introduce the Bible *in its entirety*. He helpfully sets this out under five headings that we shall take as five biblical principles to help us develop a Christian mind—a mind diametrically different from that of the secular, pagan and multi-faith world around us.

God and creation

We begin with a steadfast belief in God, a personal God and a transcendent God; a God outside everything, almighty, omniscient, omnipresent and holy; a sovereign God, who does all things according to the counsel of his own will; a God who is the living God, to whom all majesty belongs; a God who in the beginning created the heavens and the earth and all things therein. We find this teaching right through the Bible, but especially in the first book of Genesis. God, the great God of wonders, *exists*. That is the starting point—'In the beginning God . . .'

Once we take a firm stand on this truth, we are immediately at odds with the modern world to which we belong. Why is this?

First of all, because this is a world of many religions, and the modern standpoint is that they differ very little from one another. All faiths lead to the same place in the end, so you choose the one that suits you best. Moreover, most of the eastern religions hold to what is known theologically as pantheism—the belief maintained, for example, by Hinduism, that the creation is God, and God is the creation. To believe in a personal, transcendent God, a being apart from the world, and the creator of that world, is to cut across the whole thinking process of these religions.

In the second place, it is a world dominated by the scientific understanding of the beginning of things. From the standpoint of humanism and the secular mind, the favoured principle is chance. Everything has happened by chance. The universe came into being by chance; evolution occurred by chance. When we say we believe in a Creator-God, we must of necessity come into conflict

24

with this standpoint. It is a battle, and we cannot compromise or agree. We are set apart; our mind view is different.

How does belief in a Creator-God affect the believer's conduct? Once we are convinced that there is but one God, and he is the only one that merits worship, we are not going to attend services where other gods are worshipped. We are going to say, 'No, I'm jealous for my God, and that affects the way I live.' There is a renewal here, a spiritual and Christian radicalism.

In addition, we thank God for his blessings, seeing him as one with a gracious, open hand, who gives us everything. And like the people who champion green issues, we respect his creation, though not for the same reasons. Theirs often stem from other religions and the concept of Mother Earth, while we respect the created world because it is the creation of God, because he has sovereignty over all things. We obey him because he is God.

Man and the Fall

This is the second great principle that must rule our thinking. We believe that man has been created in the image of God and is therefore the pinnacle of God's creation. Man has creative ability. He is able to compose excellent poetry and great music; he is capable of the technological wizardry that enables him to go to the moon and probe the vastness of outer space. He is responsible for his life before God.

We also believe in a historic fall into sin, when our first forefather Adam failed to obey God's precise instructions. There was rebellion against God and sin came in, so that the wonderful creature became a fallen creature, deserving the death that God had warned would follow disobedience. This sin has been passed on genetically from generation to generation. We sin because we are sinners, and are not sinners because we sin. Since we are responsible to God we can be punished for our sin, and the punishment is death, physical, spiritual and eternal.

25

Does this dominate your thinking? You may hear someone say of non-Christian neighbours, 'They're lovely people.' Do you think, 'Yes, they are lovely people, but they're going to hell'? That's Christian thinking. Any other view has been influenced by the world's mindset.

The doctrine of the Fall is in total opposition to the concept of evolution, seen as a hypothesis which explains the whole of life. There is evolution within species and we cannot deny it, but when it is put forward to us as a principle which tells us where everything has come from, we say, 'There has been a Fall.' Human life is not the upward progression the evolutionists talk of, but a downward movement.

This teaching also tells us that life is holy from conception to death. This brings us into conflict with those who support abortion and euthanasia. We also believe that all human beings are to be respected, whatever their colour, sexuality, language and status. No one can be blamed for what they are, only for what they do with what they are. This applies to the 'gay' community. We have to love them as human beings. If they behave in a particular way we have to oppose it, but we don't blame them for what they are. There is to be no discrimination. The Christian is not to discriminate against any human being, for all are sinners before God and in need of grace.

We also believe in the moral law. We believe that man as a sinner will sin and is therefore in need of authority and discipline. God in his wisdom has set two great bounds for human wickedness: the family and the state.

We believe that the family unit of father, mother and children is part of God's plan from the beginning. We will love and help those who are in 'single-parent families'. They are suffering because of the sins of mankind, but it is not what God intended. We believe that the state was established by God, and that one of its duties is to reward the good and punish the evil. We support the state when it does that, and oppose it when it doesn't. The Christian who believes in the fall of mankind will, of necessity, be pro family, pro the legal system and pro good government, because this is taught by God's Word.

Our mindset is different from that of the world. We stand for what God teaches us in his Word.

The coming of Christ

For the Christian, this is the pinnacle, the greatest event in the history of the world. This is his most treasured belief—the coming of God's only begotten Son into the world to be the Saviour of mankind. In the Old Testament we see centuries of preparation for Christ's coming, from the choice of the nation to the ultimate choice of a virgin, Mary, as his mother. In the New Testament we have an account of his life, his teaching and his ministry, and more especially, an account of his death on the cross, his resurrection, and his ascension back into heaven.

The basic truth is this: believing on Christ is the most important thing that anyone must do whilst here on earth; in him *only* is there salvation and hope. There is hope nowhere else but in Christ; there is salvation in no other name. The Christian's renewed mind will be totally and utterly intolerant of any other viewpoint. There is but one way of salvation and one way to eternal life.

This immediately draws a line between Christianity and other world religions, including Judaism and Islam. Both the Jew and the Muslim refuse to believe that Christ is the Son of God, and that is why the Christian mind has to say, 'No, you are in error; there can be no compromise.' We are dealing here with the very essence of the Christian faith. Because we believe something totally different from what they believe, conflict is inevitable. And we must never contemplate working together. The Christian mind makes us unashamedly nonconformist, so very different from the loose 'accept all' mindset around us.

There are differences even within perceived Christianity. The Church of Rome, as we all know, is in agreement with us on many of the truths of the faith. Roman Catholics believe in the Creator-God; they believe in the doctrine of the Fall; they also believe in the person of Christ. But then comes the sticking point. How do you become a Christian? By works or by faith?

We contend that the teaching of the New Testament is that a person becomes a Christian and a member of Christ's kingdom by faith, and not by virtue of good works. There is conflict, and so when it comes to discussing church unity, Christians are once more 'awkward customers'. They *have* to be nonconformist. Their minds have been renewed, they can now see clearly, and they should be prepared to argue their case and win the day.

'Believing days'

Because the infallible Word of God tells us that the Lord Jesus Christ will come again at the end of the age, we are conscious that we are living in the period between his incarnation and his second coming, a period which can be called 'believing days'. This is the gospel age, an era in which people are challenged to believe in Christ and become members of his family here on earth; a time when the company of believers of all colours and languages is built up; the era of the church, when the image of God is restored in believers and they are recreated in the likeness of his Son, and when they become members of the local church, nurtured in the faith and receiving instruction on how to live moral lives within society.

The practical implication of this is that as members of the local church Christians serve God and work to bring others to the faith. We believe that the only reason the world continues is that the church is not complete. There is a tomorrow, not because the sun has not burnt out or because the world is not yet totally pol-luted, but because the church is not yet complete. The moment it is completed, there will be no tomorrow. The only reason for the progression of time is that the whole purpose of God to gather together his elect people has not yet been totally accomplished. This is Christian thinking and the Christian mindset.

The end of everything
History does not go on for ever. As there was a beginning, so there will be an end. This is how the Scriptures portray the end of the age: Christ returning on the clouds of heaven with great power and glory; the resurrection of the dead; Judgement Day when all will be judged; a new heaven and a new earth where righteousness will dwell and God will be all in all.

This view brings the Christian into immediate conflict with all those scientists and ecologists who have different, and differing, ideas about the end of this world. But we must live in the light of the Bible's agenda for the termination of things, whatever the scholars might say. Christ's parables concerning the end show us clearly what manner of people we ought to be as we live our lives here, not knowing when that great and glorious day will arrive.

A 'game plan'

Those, then, are the five things that form the Christian mind. If we are to out-think the world, we have to know what the people of the world are thinking, and we have to develop our arguments and beat them on their own ground. That is the starting point; there is no hope otherwise. In rugby terms, we must have a game plan before we start to attack the enemy and win the day.

The Christian mind starts with the Bible. Its contents, from cover to cover, must have authority over our minds. Our entire thinking process must operate within its glorious guidelines. Suddenly we might find ourselves in a discussion on some topical, contentious moral issue, and we ask ourselves, 'What should I say here? They have good arguments, how can I answer them?' It is then that we remind ourselves that we believe in God and the creation, man and the Fall, the coming of Christ, believing days and the end of everything. And we use these principles to contend for the faith. We out-think our neighbour, our family member, our work colleague; we undermine their thinking about the world; we show that it is totally false and that there is only one way of explaining the whole of existence—that found in the Bible. And we'll get there by being students of the Word and devouring its teaching.

The first step towards winning our land to Christ is the development of a Christian mind.

2
The realm
of preaching

In order to deal with this theme, let us take as a text Paul's words in his epistle to the Romans:

> That is why I am so eager to preach the gospel also to you who are at Rome. I am not ashamed of the gospel, because it is the power of God for the salvation of everyone who believes: first for the Jew, then for the Gentile (Romans 1:15-16).

When we speak of 'out-preaching', we are not merely thinking about the man in the pulpit and his forty-minute address. That is not what the Bible means by preaching. The Greek word means 'proclamation', and this includes all manner of communication where words are used—from pulpit to radio broadcast to conversation with one's neighbour.

It is abundantly clear that it is our prerogative as evangelical Christians to share our faith with others, to preach the gospel. I need hardly remind you of the great commission given by Jesus Christ to the eleven at the end of his earthly ministry:

> Therefore go and make disciples of all nations, baptising them in the name of the Father and of the Son and of the Holy Spirit, and teaching them to obey everything I have commanded you. And surely I am with you always, to the very end of the age (Matthew 28:19-20).

Peter, too, in his first epistle, tells us that we ought always to be ready to give a reason for the hope that is in us, with gentleness and respect (1 Peter 3:15). We are to be evangelistic people.

We all agree with the principle, but we have to confess that our efforts to share the gospel have not been a startling success. We look back over the last half-century, and although we have much to be thankful to God for—there has been preaching, there have been conversions, in our churches, in conventions, in camps—I am sure we would all agree that what we have seen is but the dew. We have not yet seen the showers—hundreds, thousands, yes, tens of thousands of conversions. If we want to win the country to Christ, we must win the day in the realm of preaching, proclaiming and witnessing.

The tragedy is that we are seeing other groups of zealous and dedicated people fearlessly declaring their thoughts, opinions and convictions, and steadily gaining ground. In the last twenty years the 'gay' movement has been resoundingly successful at promoting its point of view in our society. In spite of being a very small minority—perhaps one per cent of the total population—'gay' men and women are seemingly carrying the day. They have effectively proclaimed their message and won over many people to their side.

A missing factor?
We are told that eight per cent of the population of Britain attend church, and two per cent claim to be evangelicals. Yet we are not winning the day in the realm of proclamation. We know little of the success of the first three centuries, when the first believers out-preached, out-proclaimed their contemporaries.

What, then, is the answer to our problem? I need hardly remind you that our tendency as evangelicals is to argue amongst ourselves, and that the two sides in any argument tend to become polarised.

On the one hand, there are those of a more reformed persuasion who contend that there is but one answer. There must be a revival; there must be an outpouring of the Holy Spirit; we must pray to this end. That is all we can do, they say; there is no point in doing anything else. Revival is the one and only answer; let us therefore devote ourselves to prayer.

On the other hand, there are those perhaps of a more charismatic persuasion who contend that we must *do* something. The commission, they say, is 'Go', not pray and wait. We must be active. We need to discover new strategies. We need to employ new methods. We must be relevant; we must be contemporary. We must go and do something.

And yet neither side is succeeding. It seems that whichever side you are on, you are not enjoying sweeping success. And so we ask the question, What is wrong?

Let me pose another question: Have both sides lost sight of something? Have they missed something much more basic? Is there a missing factor that is common to both?

Paul's motivation

Returning to that text from Romans 1, we note that Paul says, 'I am so eager to preach the gospel also to you who are at Rome. I am not ashamed of the gospel, because it is the power of God for the salvation of everyone who believes.' In other words, Paul was consumed by a desire to preach the gospel in Rome; he was a man anxious to do something.

Let us pause for a moment to consider this man Paul. Some time around middle age he caught the travel bug; suddenly he took it into his head to set off on long journeys through Asia Minor and parts of Europe. Before that, we presume, he had been quite content with life in the university of Jerusalem. But suddenly he had 'itchy feet', and we find that he travelled thousands of miles from city to city, from country to country, from continent to continent. There were no jumbo jets, no cars, no trains, not even a bicycle—and yet off he went, on foot or by ship. In Lystra and Derbe he faced comparatively uncultured pagans. In Athens he stood before pagans who were sophisticated and more philosophically minded. And now he expresses a desire to face the political pagans of the mighty metropolis of Rome.

What was this new driving force in Paul's life? Why was he willing to confront all manner of difficulties and dangers? He faced storms at sea and robberies on land. He was scourged, thrown into prison and, once, left for dead. Yet he continued to travel, untiring and resolute.

Who was this Paul? For the early part of his life he had been one of Professor Gamaliel's ablest students at Jerusalem's university. A man with bright career prospects within Judaism, he was expected to make a name for himself and to be ranked among the Jewish greats. Doubtless, he was a genius. He could easily have stayed at home in a comfortable study in Tarsus, or in the university library in Jerusalem writing theological books. But we find him tirelessly travelling the world, and longing to visit Rome!

What was his motivation? What was the driving force that led him to say, 'I am so eager to preach the gospel also to you who are at Rome'? And who would want to go to Rome in those days? It was in the Rome of Paul's day that the seeds of the destruction of the Roman Empire were sown. Augustus Caesar was making himself a god. Claudius, who followed him, was given over to all kinds of immorality. There was incest in the royal family, and immorality, paganism and corruption in all classes of society. And yet Paul says, 'I want to go to Rome.'

But our text does not end with Paul's eagerness to go. He tells us *why* he wants to go. 'I am so eager to *preach*'—I have something I want to tell the people of Rome.

'But', you might argue, 'who among the Romans will want to listen to what you, a Jew, have to say? Your motherland,

Palestine, is but a narrow, sun-scorched strip, its people scattered worldwide. As a person you are far from imposing. There are those who have presence and can stand before an audience; they have that authority, that charisma, which enables them to communicate effectively. But not you. And what about your rhetoric? Many a great orator has gone to Rome and made a fool of himself, and you can hardly be considered a public speaker of note. Did you not confess to the Corinthians that you had not come to them "with eloquence or superior wisdom", but that you came "in weakness and fear, and with much trembling" (1 Corinthians 2:1,3)? Paul, you will surely be the laughing-stock of Rome!'

'I'm not worried about that', says Paul.

'But, Paul, the odds are stacked against you. You're going to a place where there are great thinkers, great orators. What makes you think they will listen to you?'

'It's not me. It's what I have to *say* they will listen to. I'm eager to preach *the gospel*. It's not me but the message that will make people sit up and listen. I'm proud of the message. I'm not ashamed of the gospel. I consider it the best message that this world will ever hear. I'm eager to preach it in Rome.'

And Paul makes the same point at the end of his letter to the Galatians: 'May I never boast except in the cross of our Lord Jesus Christ' (Galatians 6:14).

Confidence
Why does Paul say 'I am not ashamed of' rather than 'I am proud of' the gospel? Could it be that there were some Christians in Rome who were a little ashamed of what they believed, and were reluctant to speak openly lest they be thought odd or considered fanatics by their neighbours or workmates? Were they afraid of how people might react to what they believed, and as a result had they lost some confidence in what this message could accomplish in those who didn't believe it? Not so Paul. He declares, 'I am not

35

ashamed of the gospel.' I have good news, a message I want the people of Rome to hear. I'm proud of that message. It's my boast. I glory in it.

I wonder if it is similarly true to say that our lack of success in the realm of proclamation and witnessing has to do with the fact that we also have lost sight of the glory of the gospel we possess? Perhaps, because of the age in which we live, there has surreptitiously crept into our churches and into our minds an element of embarrassment, causing us to lose confidence in the gospel.

We can become conditioned when we are continually battered by atheism. We have read about the attacks that are made on the gospel, the insistence that there is no absolute truth, that truth is relative. 'You follow your religion,' we are told, 'and we will follow ours. Something may be true for you, something else may be true for us.'

We have seen the decline and relative ineffectiveness of the gospel in our day, and our confidence in it is shaken and doubt creeps in. There are people who call us fanatics, and we do not wish to be odd. Neither do we want people to consider us fools; we prefer to be accepted and respected. We want the media to think well of us, and so we refrain from 'telling it as it is'. Perhaps we are a little ashamed, and once we begin to waver, any impetus or drive to witness to others dampens down and we begin to lose confidence in the gospel itself.

Maybe this is the more basic problem, the factor that is true of reformed and charismatic people alike. Maybe this is part of the reason why we are not winning the day in preaching and proclamation. If we do not have a hundred per cent confidence in the message we have to proclaim, we will never win the day in the realm of preaching

Paul did not have this problem. He could say, 'I am so eager to preach the gospel also to you who are in Rome. I am not ashamed of the gospel.' He was full of confidence and vigour, his pride and his boast were in the good news he had to share.

The message

Well, what was this message? What was it in this message that gave Paul such glorious confidence and overpowering joy when facing the pagan farmers of Lystra, the pagan philosophers of Athens, the pagan politicians of Rome, the sexual perverts of Corinth, and any other living person? Would not understanding this message, and knowing what it was, make giants of us also? What exactly was it?

The answer is very simple. Paul says, 'I am not ashamed of the *gospel*.' His message is news, good news, the good news about Jesus Christ.

Remarkable news

Jesus Christ was a Jew, born about forty years earlier in Bethlehem of Judea. What is so wonderful about that? The answer is that Jesus Christ was the only begotten Son of God—that, surely, is good news!

A son born to Caesar in Rome would cause quite a stir in the city. Another son for Caesar! The imperial heralds would announce that son's birth. But Paul was heralding the coming of the Son of God into the world, and if the birth of a son to Caesar was good news, he had greater, better and more wonderful news. The message I have, says Paul, is that the Son of God has come into the world.

This is how one Welsh hymnist viewed that coming:

> *Of all the wonders wrought in heaven*
> *The greatest was the plan*
> *That the immortal Son divine*
> *Become a mortal man.*

37

Are you absolutely convinced of this truth? We will not out-preach unless we are! Paul was convinced, and he was filled with a burning desire to share this good news, which had been revealed to him by the Saviour himself, not only with his fellow Jews but with Gentiles also. The people of Athens and Corinth and Rome must be told; someone must go to those cities with the glorious news of the birth of the Son of God. Paul had no option but to go personally; he was constrained by an overwhelming sense of love and gratitude to God.

It was indeed a wonderful story that Paul had to share. The Son of God had come into the world, born miraculously in a lowly stable in Bethlehem and welcomed by a choir of angels—such a choir as had never graced the birth of a son of Caesar!—proclaiming jubilantly, 'Glory to God in the highest'.

When this babe had grown to manhood, and was being baptised in the Jordan, a dove came upon him and the voice of God spoke the astonishing words, 'You are my Son, whom I love; with you I am well pleased' (Mark 1:11). Then he began his ministry, travelling around the country. He turned water into wine, gave sight to the blind, healed the sick and even raised the dead. But he went to the cross, was buried in a grave, was resurrected on the third day, and within forty days was taken back into heaven. What a strange and wonderful story! The Son of God had lived on this earth for thirty-three years, and had then returned to his Father in heaven. What news!

Are we as moved by the wonder of the gospel as Paul was? He was so taken up with it that he could not but share it with others. He said: 'People must know; at all costs I must go and tell them. I must get to Rome to tell even those in Caesar's household that the Son of God has come.'

Are we ashamed of the news that the Son of God has come into the world? Why are we so quiet? If we are to win this land for Christ, the first thing we have to do is see that people hear the gospel. We must realise that in this day and age the majority know very little about Jesus Christ, and few have heard the good news proclaimed.

The task, you might say, is insurmountable—an impossibility. But were not the people of Athens and Rome just as ignorant and antagonistic when Paul arrived in their midst? Up to that point, they had not heard a word of this God-Man, Jesus Christ; but the apostle saw to it that they did not remain in their ignorance. Despite the fact that the people ridiculed him and the philosophers mocked him, Paul told them that the Son of God had come into the world, that he had been crucified on Calvary, that he had risen from the grave on the third day and ascended into heaven. Paul says, 'I am not ashamed of the gospel.'

Relevant news

The news that Paul was eager to share was also relevant. He says, 'I am not ashamed of the gospel, because it is the power of God for the *salvation* of everyone who believes.' It was relevant then, and it is relevant now. The Son of God had come into the world to save. Had not the angels proclaimed that they had tidings of great joy? 'Today in the town of David a Saviour has been born to you.' A Saviour—one who provides salvation!

But salvation from what? Well, from sin. Although we have crossed the threshold into the twenty-first century, the modern man is still trying to solve the problem of what is wrong with mankind. For Christians, it is an accepted fact that we have some inherent weakness, that there is some flaw in our make-up, that we have a tendency to do what we know we should not be doing. There are those who can, to varying degrees, control their wilful tendencies, but we are all culpable. We all tell the occasional lie, we lose our temper, we envy, we covet. And in some people the grossest of sins come to the surface, and they are seen to be thieves, adulterers and murderers. When the Fall occurred, sin came into the world, and it continues to cause problems for individuals, for families, for nations and, indeed, for the world.

Sin, in the first place, gives us a guilty conscience; it causes inner unease. Now this modern age hankers after the very opposite—what is termed inner peace or tranquillity. That is why people flock to therapists and counsellors. There are so many complications in their lives that they are agitated and restless and cannot sleep at night. Why? Their conscience is pricking them. They need healing. But this condition is beyond therapy; it calls for the skill of the Great Physician.

In the second place, this sin, this wickedness that affects us personally, affects other people around us. If we sin, someone else is bound to suffer. If a husband is unfaithful to his wife, the trauma for her and the children is indescribable. If someone breaks into a house and steals, there is not only sadness at the loss of personal property but a strange feeling of contamination. If a drunken driver kills a child, the whole family is smitten with grief and despair. Sins cause sadness and heartbreak. The depth of despair in people's hearts reflects the suffering caused not only by their own sins but by the sins of others. A bomb explodes in Northern Ireland and innocent lives are lost or irreparably damaged, and the age-old question is asked: How is it that people can do such things?

In the third place, there is a holy God who, on Judgement Day, will weigh each individual in the balance and, in his righteousness, will punish sin. There is a place of eternal punishment, a place of utter darkness where there is wailing and gnashing of teeth, a place of everlasting fire.

The people around us need salvation. We have only to step back to see the sadness, the agony, the worry, the hopelessness and the darkness of our generation.

Paul knew that this was the sad condition of the people of Rome, and his words are, 'That is why I am so eager to preach the gospel.' Why? Because he had news, wonderful news, to tell. The Son of God had come into the world to save sinners. He had come on a mission of salvation. The Son of God had died on the cross so that guilty consciences could be forgiven, so that the power of sin in their lives could be broken and they no longer had to harvest its blasted crop and face hell and the eternal punishment of God.

With such wonderful news to share, Paul was unashamed. The very thought that the Son of God had come into the world for the sole purpose of saving sinners thrilled his soul and set his heart ablaze, and he declares, 'I am eager to preach the gospel'—yes, in Rome.

Are we ashamed of the gospel of Christ? Is it not just as relevant today as it was in Rome in the first century? Is salvation not just as imperative in our land today as it was in Athens, Rome and Corinth in days of old? If it was man's only hope then, it remains man's only hope today.

Powerful news

Let us move forward a step. Why was Paul going to Rome with the gospel of Jesus Christ? It was remarkable news, it was relevant news, but it was also powerful news. He writes, 'It is the *power of God* for the salvation of everyone who believes.' The message is 'the power'. What does Paul mean by this?

In the first place, Paul is saying that this gospel is God's way of doing things and is therefore powerful. Over the centuries man has been trying to solve the problem of sin. Educationalists, philosophers, psychologists have all tried to help, but all their efforts have been in vain.

But this gospel I wish to share with you, says Paul, reveals the power of God. The power of God who is the creator and sustainer of all the cosmos; the one who promised Adam and Eve that the woman's seed would one day crush the head of the serpent; the one who inspired Isaiah to say that the Suffering Servant would be led as a lamb to the slaughter and, as a sheep before its shearers is silent, so he would not open his mouth; the one who chose the Virgin Mary to be his Son's earthly mother; the one who was there when the holy babe was born in Bethlehem, when the heavenly dove descended upon him at his baptism in the waters of Jordan, when the raging sea was calmed, when the water was turned into wine, when the blind man's eyes were opened; the one whose mighty power was at work on resurrection day—his power for salvation is at work in the proclamation of the gospel.

But there is even more to it than that. Paul does not say that the gospel of Christ *tells* us about God's power for salvation, but that the gospel *is* God's power for salvation. Do we believe this when we talk to our neighbours? We are not merely passing on remarkable news, not even good news; but as we speak, the power of God is there in the message.

Now this is where we are faced with a slight theological problem. In 1 Thessalonians 1:5 Paul says, 'because our gospel came to you not simply with words, but also with power, with the Holy Spirit and with deep conviction'. And again in 2 Corinthians 3:6 he says, 'He has made us competent as ministers of a new covenant—not of the letter but of the Spirit; for the letter kills, but the Spirit gives life.' Is not Paul here contradicting himself? In Romans he says that the gospel is the power of God, and yet in 1 Thessalonians he says that the gospel can be in word only and not in the Spirit. On the one hand he is saying that the power of God is in the message, and on the other hand that the message can be ineffective. How are we to reconcile these two things?

In his volumes of sermons on Romans, Dr Martyn Lloyd-Jones makes an invaluable contribution when it comes to understanding Romans 1:16. Dealing with the word 'power', he says that it is possible to translate the original Greek word as 'prescription'. 'I am not ashamed of the gospel, because it is the *prescription* of

God for the salvation of everyone who believes.' Then, being himself a medical man, he develops the picture. When you have an ailment you go to the doctor, and he makes a diagnosis and hands you a prescription. What is the prescription? Well, it is nothing but a fragile piece of paper, a written note. And yet it has wonderful power, because that prescription is your remedy—there is life in the written words. If you take it to the chemist the remedy will be released to you. So it is with the gospel. It is possible for the gospel to be 'in word only'—the prescription—and yet in the word there is power, power for salvation.

There are many scriptures that speak of the intrinsic power of the gospel. In 1 Corinthians 1:21 we read that 'God was pleased through the foolishness of what was preached to save those who believe.' And Peter tells the scattered pilgrims that they have been born again 'not of perishable seed, but of imperishable, through *the living and enduring word of God*' (1 Peter 1:23). That is, the gospel is the means of conversion; in it there is power that can regenerate people.

Something similar is found in verse 18 of the first chapter of James' epistle: 'He chose to give us birth through the word of truth.' That is, God begets people by the proclamation of the gospel. There is power at work, and it is effective. The gospel is God's way of doing things, and it is invincible.

Paul says: When I am proclaiming this message in Rome, God will also be at work; his power will be at work in the message. Had Paul not proved that to be true in Corinth? We are familiar with his words in 1 Corinthians 2:

When I came to you, brothers, I did not come with eloquence or superior wisdom as I proclaimed to you the testimony about God. For I resolved to know nothing while I was with you except Jesus Christ and him crucified. I came to you in weakness and fear, and with much trembling. My message and my

43

preaching were not with wise and persuasive words, but with a demonstration of the Spirit's power (verses 1-4).

That is why Paul was not ashamed of the gospel of Christ.

'Everyone who believes'

We have all, I feel sure, heard this news. Perhaps there is some-one saying, 'Yes, ever since childhood I've known the story about the Son of God coming into the world.' Perhaps there is someone saying for the first time, 'I'm beginning to see that it is good news *for me*. Not just good news for sinners in general, but good news for me as a sinner.' Perhaps there is someone who has seen his sin and realises that this message of Paul is especially relevant. Perhaps, as you read this, you realise that something strange is happening in your soul—that there is a power at work, that you are beginning to feel differently about things and beginning to see things anew. Perhaps you are asking, 'What shall I do that I might be saved?'

'I am not ashamed of the gospel, because it is the power of God for the salvation of *everyone* who believes.' It is for you today if you are ready to believe. Believe in the Lord Jesus Christ. Believe in the Son of God, that he came down from heaven to earth. Believe in salvation, in the good news that he died to take away your sins. And believe also that there is a great power at work in your soul, that will gloriously finish the work one day in eternity.

In Romans 8, when Paul has completed his explanation of the gospel in its fullness, he says with absolute confidence:

For I am convinced that neither death nor life, neither angels nor demons, neither the present nor the future, nor any powers, neither height nor depth, nor anything else in all creation, will be able to separate us from the love of God that is in Christ Jesus our Lord (verses 38-39).

Small wonder that he is not ashamed of the gospel! Nothing will prevail against its almighty power. Nothing will prevent its work for the salvation of everyone who believes.

This great gospel!

Yes, we need revival, and we need to be contemporary. But first and foremost we need to be convinced that we have the most wonderful, the most powerful, the most effective and the most marvellous message that the world has ever heard—and that God himself is in it. We must pray for the blessing of God's Spirit, but we must restore our confidence in the excellence of the message that we have to proclaim. And when we see its excellence, we too will catch Paul's energy and enthusiasm, and there will be no stopping our telling and proclaiming.

Paul says that he is not ashamed of the gospel and he is ready to declare it even in Rome. Where is our Rome? Is it our work-place, our neighbours, our family? We might say, 'They're beyond the pale.' Paul might have said that about the Rome of his day, but instead he said: 'I'm eager to go to Rome because I've got this message. I'm nothing. I have no powers of oratory, I'm nothing to look at, but I've got this message which is the power of God for salvation. It can turn the world upside down, and the people of Rome are going to hear it.'

That is how the church of the first centuries out-preached the world. It wasn't strategy; it was a conviction of the power of the message. And this is the second step towards winning our country to Christ. We are to preach this great gospel, which is the power of God for the salvation of everyone who believes.

3
The realm
of love

The Bible is full of exhortations with respect to love. The Lord Jesus Christ himself tells us that there are only two great commandments, and they both involve love: in the first place, loving God, and then loving one's neighbour as oneself. And both the Gospels and the Epistles emphasise the fact that Christians should love their fellow Christians.

In John 13:34 we find Jesus telling his disciples that they are to obey a new, and more demanding, commandment to love: 'A new command I give you: Love one another. As I have loved you, so you must love one another.' And he repeats this exhortation in John 15:12, 'My command is this: Love each other as I have loved you.' This love, of itself, would be a testimony: 'By this all men will know that you are my disciples, if you love one another' (John 13:35).

To judge from the evidence of Scripture, the world did indeed know this. The testimony of the early Christians to the unbelieving world around them was astonishing and dramatic, so that the world marvelled, 'See how they love one another!' (Words spoken by the opponents of Christianity in the first century, quoted by the early Christian writer Tertullian.)

In his first epistle, John repeatedly exhorts his 'little children' to continue loving. 'This is the message you heard from the beginning: We should love one another' (1 John 3:11). Again, in verse 23 he says, 'And this is his command: to believe in the name of his Son, Jesus Christ, and to love one another as he commanded us'; and in 1 John 4:7 he says, 'Dear friends, let us love one another, for love comes from God.' Paul, too, in each of his epistles, bids the brethren love one another, and in Galatians 5:22 he reminds them that love is a fruit of the Spirit.

The imperative of love

The frequent occurrence of the exhortation to love is significant. If God's Word but once commands something, we are expected to obey; but if it is does so time and time again, it is imperative that we do so. God, in his wisdom, when inspiring men to write the Scriptures, saw to it that this exhortation was repeated regularly and often. Let us now consider why he chose to do this.

I am sure that children often get tired of hearing their parents constantly telling them to do this or not to do that. But why is it that parents repeatedly warn their children about certain things? There are two reasons: in the first place, it is because parents are not sure that they have been heard the first time; and in the second place, because what they have to say is of the greatest importance. God, being the Father of believers, deals with us as children, and he too repeats himself. Why? In case we have not heard the first time, and because what he has to say is of vital importance: love one another.

A year or so ago, at a service held in Carmarthen to launch the Welsh version of his book *O! Ryfedd Ras* (*Oh! Wondrous Grace*), J. Elwyn Davies, the first General Secretary of the Evangelical Movement of Wales, was asked to give a brief account of the birth of the Movement. During his résumé of the early years, he said that his abiding memory was of an overwhelming spirit of fellowship and companionship between the brothers and sisters—a relationship pervaded with a deep love for one another. Then, looking around at the friends gathered together to pay tribute to his wise leadership over a long period of time, he earnestly pleaded, 'My dear friends, love one another.' Sitting among those friends, and having already decided on the third theme of this address, I was conscious not only of God's confirmation but also that he was telling me how important it is to love the brethren.

Love for fellow believers

We do not have to think hard to see the relevance of this theme in our day. It is relevant to our relationship one with another as believers in the church. Many Christians know what it is to be hurt by their fellow Christians. A Christian somewhere has failed to love as he ought, and we have been wounded. Conversely, there are others whom we have failed to love; we have hurt them by something we have said or the way we have dealt with them. And this lack of love manifests itself in disagreements and divisions, and in people leaving churches and new churches being set up.

It seems to me that there are two areas in which we are particularly prone to failure to love one another, and where strife and divisions occur.

Secondary matters

We are agreed on the basic doctrines, the great foundations of our faith, but we often disagree profoundly on secondary matters. There are many issues in the Bible and many aspects of church life on which the most godly of believers take opposing views. And there is nothing at all wrong with disagreement between those who adopt one or other of the various opinions. The vital question is: What spirit pervades the argument and consequent disagreement? Do we disagree in love?

We must confess that we have not always been successful here. The secondary doctrinal matter becomes so important to us that we cannot cope with anyone who disagrees with us. We become entrenched, resentful and argumentative, and love disappears out of the door, along with the offended believer. All too often this is the spirit seen in church meetings.

Personality clashes
We thank God that we are not all the same, but it is sometimes difficult to work alongside people of a certain disposition, and this can cause tension and lead to disagreement. Personality clashes are often an even greater problem than differences over secondary doctrinal matters. The problem was not unknown in the early church. The book of Acts truthfully records such clashes between Paul and Barnabas, and Paul and Peter; but they were temporary, and settled amicably, and love was in evidence.

When love fails
It is small wonder, then, that the Scripture exhorts us to love. God knew there would be problems concerning matters of secondary importance, and he also knew there would be many a clash of personalities. 'Love one another!' The exhortation is relevant to us today; for when love fails, the consequence is disastrous for the church in the world.

What happens to a church in which such disputes occur? The first thing is that the church stops growing and goes into a backwater for a while. Everyone is taken up with the big controversy. The church forgets that there is an unsaved world outside; it is constantly looking inwards and not outwards; the minister's thinking is dominated by the problem, and the prayer meeting is no longer focused on the lost. The devil smiles, for he knows that Britain will never be won for Christ if this lack of love continues. How relevant this theme is! We need to learn love.

Love for non-Christians
This exhortation is relevant not only to us as fellow Christians, but just as much to our relationship with the world around us.

For, as we know, Scripture urges us not only to love those who are members of God's church, but also our neighbour, whether within the church or 'in the world'. The charge has been made against evangelicals that we have failed to love the world.

Physical needs

We are accused of loving the soul more than the body, of being more concerned with sending missionaries to proclaim the Word than with feeding the starving. Certainly, if we are to love our neighbour as ourselves, this will include caring for the whole person and not just responding to spiritual needs. We are to be noted for our good works; indeed, 'we are . . . created in Christ Jesus to do good works' (Ephesians 2:10). We are to be in the forefront of any battle against injustice in society. We should take up the cause of the weak and those who cannot speak up for themselves. And we must be prepared to own up if we have failed.

But it is surely true to say that we are now beginning to regain a correct balance in this matter. The development of Tear Fund and of similar societies has seen the pendulum swing steadily towards the centre. I sincerely hope that it will not swing too far in the opposite direction. Keeping the pendulum in the centre position is a constant challenge.

Intolerance

Sometimes people say to us, 'Since God is love, how can you claim to be God's children and yet be so intolerant?' To the man of the world, love and intolerance are irreconcilable. Tolerance is seen as the number one virtue. Every sin is forgiven except that of intolerance. We live in a multi-faith, multi-cultural society, and we are told that if we want to live in harmony we have to tolerate every religious and moral stance—we must all get on together.

More often than not, we are not too sure how to deal with this accusation. How do we reconcile intolerance with love?

Part of the answer to this accusation is that tolerance is a very feeble virtue; there is nothing at all robust about it. Tolerance is getting on with everybody and agreeing with everything; tolerance is closing your eyes to everything you don't like; tolerance costs nothing. But we have been called to a higher virtue: 'Love your neighbour as yourself.' And that must be our answer to those who accuse us—true love is essentially intolerant.

Think for a minute of a newly married couple who have vowed to love one another until death. Suddenly there appears another man who tries to entice the wife away from her husband. Does that husband show tolerance? Does he shut his eyes to what is happening? Not at all. Because of his love, he will be intolerant. He will not allow such a thing to happen.

Again, take parents and children. Parents can be intolerant. Why? Because they love their children. They do not want them to be harmed in any way, and so they will not tolerate any threat that may cross their paths.

Love desires the best for its object; it is unwilling to settle for anything less. Love your neighbour *as yourself.* We all want the best for ourselves, and so we want the best for our neighbour. It is because of this love that we are intolerant of all other religions— they do not offer our neighbour what Christianity has to offer. Whilst we should love the followers of every religion, we must be utterly intolerant of the religion itself.

Paul felt this intolerance when he arrived in Athens. We are told that 'he was greatly distressed to see that the city was full of idols' (Acts 17:16). Why? He was jealous for the glory of God. His heart was ablaze; he must do something. 'So he reasoned in the synagogue . . . as well as in the market-place day by day' (Acts 17:17). When we have strong feelings, we do something, do we not? Controlling his feelings, Paul moved to the sphere of the mind and reasoned with his hearers. The good news about Jesus Christ had to be presented to the minds of these people. Paul was intolerant of what he was seeing around him because he had something much better to offer.

The same is true when it comes to morals. Christian love is intolerant of any kind of immorality, because it cheapens and destroys human life. Love, in its essence, is far loftier than tolerance.

Therefore, when we are accused of being intolerant, we need not be ashamed, nor need we feel that there is anything wrong with our Christianity. Our love ascends to a much higher plane—desiring the best for people—and we have to be intolerant of that which is base and degrading. In a society where the best that can be offered is tolerance, the field is wide open for us to out-love the world.

In the midst of this tolerant society people are crying out to be loved. This is a society in which marriages are breaking up, children are being pulled all ways, merciless bosses are getting rid of workers with impunity, and countless numbers are lonely and longing for someone to love them, someone to appreciate them and respect them as people. The battle is there to be won.

The supremacy of love

When we consider the numerous Christian virtues applauded in the Bible, we may ask, Why this great emphasis on love? If we turn to the first epistle of John we find the aged apostle setting down the reasons why love is of primary importance. First,

Dear friends, I am not writing you a new command but an old one, which you have had since the beginning. This old command is the message you have heard. Yet I am writing you a new command; its truth is seen in him and you, because the darkness is passing and the true light is already shining (2:7-8).

We have been given a *command*, and a command 'since the beginning'. That is one reason why love is so important. This is a low-level reason: we are to love one another because we are commanded by God to do so.

In 1 John 3:11-16 John's reasoning reaches a higher plane:

> This is the message you heard from the beginning: We should love one another. Do not be like Cain, who belonged to the evil one and murdered his brother . . . We know that we have passed from death to life, because we love our brothers (verses 11-12, 14).

Love, says John, emanates from the fact that we have moved from death to life. Then he writes:

> Anyone who hates his brother is a murderer, and you know that no murderer has eternal life in him. This is how we know what love is: Jesus Christ laid down his life for us. And we ought to lay down our lives for our brothers (verses 15-16).

We have received love, argues John, love that was so costly. Therefore we should be prepared to show the same love to one another.

Then, thirdly, John moves his argument to the highest possible level:

> Dear friends, let us love one another, for love comes from God. Everyone who loves has been born of God and knows God. Whoever does not love does not know God, because God is love (1 John 4:7-8).

If we are the children of God, then we are to reproduce the characteristics of our heavenly Father. The presence of love proves that we are born of God, while the absence of love shows that we are not born of God, because God is love.

Could it be that the number of Christians is fewer than the number of evangelicals? You can have an evangelical profession, evangelical doctrine and an evangelical lifestyle, but if love is missing they count for nothing. John is saying here that if we are members of God's family, and our Father by his very nature is love, then we, his children, will be of the same nature. We are members of the family of love.

John continues:

> This is how God showed his love among us: He sent his one and only Son into the world that we might live through him. This is love: not that we loved God, but that he loved us and sent his Son as an atoning sacrifice for our sins. Dear friends, since God so loved us, we also ought to love one another (verses 9-11).

Not only is love in God's nature, but he has also revealed his love in a unique way, by sending his one and only Son to this world for our salvation. How is it possible, asks John, for a person who has proved such great love *not* to love?

There is something exceedingly selfish about a person who has been the object of the grace and love that flowed on Calvary, and yet, in his own shrivelled little life, denies those very things in his dealings with his fellow Christians and the outside world. Love seeks the very best for the object of love, and in the gospel we have the supreme example of such love. God so loved the world that he gave his Son; Jesus Christ loved us so much that he gave his life for us. Why cannot we love one another if the spirit of love dwells within our hearts? Such love shown to us should humble us, move us and melt our hearts, and should express itself in love flowing to those around us.

John moves on to another important statement in verse 12: 'No-one has ever seen God; but if we love one another, God lives in us and his love is made complete in us.' How are people going to see God? How are we going to get the people of the world interested in the gospel of Christ? How will a world that does not acknowledge God be won over? John makes this astounding statement: they will see God if the love of God is manifest in us and is made complete, or fulfilled, in us. When people see this love they will want to possess it; our lives will be attractive.

This is the back-up argument to out-thinking and out-preaching the world. The revelation of love will overpower the world. It was because love was so abundantly displayed in the lives of the early Christians that the pagans around them were drawn to enquire what their secret was. Was it not said of them, 'See how these Christians love one another!'? Love is the great Christian moral virtue. It is the mark of God, and it should be the mark of his people. If we are to win the day in this land of ours, we have to win the day in the realm of love.

What is love?

But what exactly is this love? How does it work out in the daily life of the church, and in our dealings with those people we meet from day to day? To answer this, we need to look at 1 Corinthians 13, a chapter we should be thoroughly conversant with if we are going to out-love the world.

In the Greek language there are three words for love: one for sexual love, one that expresses fondness or friendship, and one (*agapë*) that is used in the New Testament to describe the love of God. Implied in the last is the meaning of desiring the best for someone—desiring the best for undeserving people, whatever the cost, in a reflection of God's love for us.

What are the practical implications of nurturing this love in our lives? Chapter 13 of 1 Corinthians is most helpful and searching in this respect. Notice how Paul closes chapter 12:

'And now I will show you the most excellent way.' You cannot get higher than this!

Paul then starts chapter 13 with negatives:

> If I speak in the tongues of men and of angels, but have not love, I am only a resounding gong or a clanging cymbal. If I have the gift of prophecy and can fathom all mysteries and all knowledge, and if I have a faith that can move mountains, but have not love, I am nothing. If I give all I possess to the poor and surrender my body to the flames, but have not love, I gain nothing (verses 1-3).

These must be among the most frightening verses in Scripture! Many wonderful things can be true of us: we can possess the tongues of men and of angels, have the gift of prophecy, acquire knowledge, penetrate mysteries, feed the poor, and even sacrifice ourselves—but all for nothing if we have no love.

It is not gifts that prove faith, but fruit. There are many Christians who, though they have very few gifts, are higher up the ladder than those with many gifts, and that is because in their lives there is much fruit—love, gentleness, meekness, kindness, sobriety. They abound in the graces of Christianity. You can be firm in your reformed doctrine, clear in your ecclesiology, uncompromising on the question of baptism, praised for practising your gifts in the church—and yet be nothing.

Patience and kindness
'*Love is patient*' (AV 'suffereth long'). Love shows great patience in relation to people who hurt us or cause us harm. And there are such people, are there not? They can deceive us, do us a bad turn, besmirch our reputation, speak maliciously of us, disparage us, ignore us. How do we respond? Often our temper is roused and we lose control of that 'small member', the tongue; we take

offence and retaliate, repaying evil for evil. And how often are we heard to say, 'I'll never forgive'! But love forgives up to seven times, yes, and up to seventy-seven times (Matthew 18:22). It is long-suffering.

Very well, you say, but what happens if someone in the church does something truly bad to me? What should I do? Turn to Scripture and you will find clear instructions on how to deal with such difficulties. 'If your brother sins against you, go and show him his fault, just between the two of you. If he listens to you, you have won your brother over' (Matthew 18:15).

So, if someone in the church harms you in any way, telling another person about it in order to gain sympathy for your cause is *not* the first step you take. You do not gather around you a clique of sympathisers but, without telling anyone else, you go immediately to the person in question in order to win your brother. You go to him in love, and if he also practises love he will listen to you in love.

But what if you do not succeed? 'But if he will not listen, take one or two others along, so that "every matter may be established by the testimony of two or three witnesses"' (verse 16). That is the way to deal with problems arising from disagreements in the church.

Peter says, 'love covers over a multitude of sins' (1 Peter 4:8). But so often we are anxious to uncover them. We are so quick to say, 'Have you heard . . .?' How prone we are to reveal each other's sins! But we are told to keep them hidden. Love is long-suffering.

In the Gospel of Luke Jesus Christ says these words: 'If your brother . . . sins against you seven times in a day, and seven times comes back to you and says, "I repent," forgive him' (Luke 17:3-4). Seven times in a day! The offender repents seven times, and you forgive him seven times. Why? Because love is patient. There is a Welsh hymn which asks, 'Is it true that you forgive me the same sin a hundred times?' That is what we expect of God, but what do we offer our brother? Love is long-suffering.

Love is '*kind*'. We all understand what that means—generosity, and offering practical help to the people around us. But it means kindness not only to fellow members of the church, but also to our enemies. Remember the words of Jesus: 'But I tell you who hear me: Love your enemies, do good to those who hate you, bless those who curse you, pray for those who ill-treat you' (Luke 6:27-28). The world cannot get hold of this philosophy, but as Christians we are to show kindness even to our enemies, those who most bitterly oppose us. We are to look for opportunities to be kind.

Love's negatives

Love '*does not envy*'. Envy is that feeling of resentment that we experience when we find that someone else is preferred above ourselves. It is that sort of zealous jealousy that shows itself in body language, words and actions. Envy stems from pride. A friend has had a promotion, and because I have been overlooked I am envious and set out to denigrate him.

But the essence of love is joy in another's success. We belong to the same body and the same kingdom, and if a Christian is promoted we all say, 'Great! That's God's will for him.' If another church is experiencing a period of blessing, we are not to be envious; rather, we are to be delighted that God's work is prospering elsewhere, despite the fact that we are perhaps battling in a very difficult situation. We rejoice because of the love that we have.

'*It . . . does not boast, it is not proud.*' Blowing one's own trumpet can reveal itself in a number of ways: pride in one's family, pride in one's job, pride in one's knowledge, pride in one's experiences, pride in success, ecclesiastical pride, doctrinal pride. And what does pride do? It exalts itself, and in so doing it drags other people down.

Love is not like that; it makes us see others as better than ourselves. Do you recall Paul's words in Philippians 2:3? 'Do nothing out of selfish ambition or vain conceit, but in humility consider others better than yourselves.' That is love: appreciating other people; seeing something good in them and, conscious of your own weaknesses, regarding them as better than yourself.

'*It is not rude.*' Love does not behave in a shameful manner. It is not arrogant, unseemly, proud and scornful. There is nothing at all indecent about the Christian's morals. Indecency can be a temptation for others—indecency of language, indecency of dress. It is not an act of love to parade temptation before the eyes of others. There is something respectable, pure and holy in the way love operates. Why? Because it desires the best for the other person; we do not want to be a hindrance to our fellow Christians. Therefore, nothing indecent must be allowed to come into our relationship with one another.

Love is '*not self-seeking*'. In this modern age, the vital question asked by so many is 'What's best for me?' The capital 'I' must come first. And this attitude is not unknown in the context of the church. A Christian may be heard to say, 'I don't seem to be getting anything in the church I belong to. I'm going to go to another one.' But what about the people who are being left behind? If everybody were to do that, there would be no members remaining. What makes you believe that you have a right to go, and that they have to remain? You are thinking of yourself, not of others: What am *I* getting? What will benefit *me*?

But what does the Christian who is ruled by love do? He remains in his church, and he loves the brethren and the sisters, despite their faults. If you feel that the minister has a problem—and we ministers do have problems—well, go to him and have a word with him in love. If you feel that the fault lies with the elders, then have a word with them in love. And if you feel that you are the only one who is right, and that all the other members are a problem, then go and have a word with them all in turn, in love!

Love is '*not easily angered*'. Have you seen people easily provoked in a church meeting? I have been to many a committee meeting where members have fallen prey to provocation and have become annoyed. And who were the members around the table? The saints! Those God loved, those Christ had died for! Love declares that such things ought not to be.

Love '*keeps no record of wrongs*' (AV 'thinketh no evil'). We ought not to judge our fellow Christians until we have incontrovertible proof that there is something radically wrong. In the meantime we must give them the benefit of the doubt; we are not to be suspicious of their motives or of their actions. Are we not often tempted to do that? But we must resist the temptation and say, 'No, I love that brother. He's a child of God.'

'*Love does not delight in evil.*' Love is grieved when news of the fall of a fellow believer is received. Like Shem and Japheth, Christians make every effort to prevent sin being exposed and passed on (Genesis 9:23).

Love's positives

Love '*always protects*' (AV 'beareth all things'). This relates not to people, but to situations that cause grief and pain. One of our problems is that we grumble so much. Just as love is long-suffering when dealing with people, so it suffers all things in terms of circumstances and events. If you continually moan about every situation that arises, you are going to be a burden to your fellow Christians. It is a sign of love that we are ready to suffer without grumbling.

'*It . . . always trusts, always hopes.*' Commentators differ in their interpretation of these two clauses. Some maintain that they refer to our relationship with each other: we are to believe the best and hope the best about one another until we have clear evidence

61

to the contrary. Others are of the opinion that they refer to our relationship with God: believing all things that are told us by God, and hoping all the things God has promised.

Love *'always perseveres'* (AV 'endureth all things'). This is not unlike the long-suffering that heads the list. But Paul is not repeating himself; here he is referring to a particular aspect of that long-suffering. The Greek word that Paul uses comes from the military world and refers to the strength to withstand the attacks of the enemy. What we have here is endurance in Christian warfare—opposing and withstanding the devil and spiritual powers. We know that the devil is like a roaring lion seeking to devour whom he will, but we are to stand firm in the battle. We are to stand together, for it is an act of love to stand shoulder to shoulder with our brethren in battle.

Of course, all wars have their 'deserters', those soldiers who run away when the heat of battle becomes too fierce; but they not only let themselves down, they let others down too. Running away is not an act of love; it is shameful to desert one's comrades. The same is true in the spiritual world. Love stands with the brethren in the heat of the battle.

The mark of heaven
'Love never fails.' Here Paul reaches the pinnacle, and the remaining verses of the chapter are taken up with explaining this statement. Put very simply, it means that love has no end, it continues to eternity. This is why love is the greatest of all Christian virtues, the very mark of heaven.

You will remember that this chapter comes in the context of spiritual gifts. Both natural and miraculous gifts were evident in the Corinthian church. They had led to pride and splits within the church, and Paul therefore reminds the church members of the more excellent way of love. It is love, and not gifts, that will keep the church together. All these gifts, Paul tells them, are only temporary. They will fail; they will cease; they will vanish away. But love excels them all, because it will continue. Spiritual gifts will not be needed in heaven; but love will continue, because heaven is a kingdom of love.

In his volume of sermons on this chapter, Jonathan Edwards entitles his concluding chapter, 'Heaven, a world of love'. The God who is love will be there; Christ, who loved his friends so much that he died for them, will be there; the Spirit of love will be there; and the saints will be there; and there they will love one another.

The power of love

We see now why we must win the day in the realm of love. Let us consider one another and encourage one another to love and good works. Needless to say, we want other Christians to love us, but we are to start by loving them. We have to admit that we often fail here. As we look around the congregation, whether it be in a Sunday service in our home church or in a conference, what we see are sinners whom God loved, whom Christ died for, and in whose hearts the Holy Spirit is at work. Ought we not to make every possible effort to love them?

Imagine yourself standing on a platform with a door on either side. One by one the members of your church cross the platform in front of you—pastor, elders, deacons, members, adherents—and as they pass, you say to each in turn, 'I love you, I love you.' Then go home and do it! If we did this, something remarkable would happen in our churches. There would be a great sense of unity, fellowship and warmth, and it would overflow into a lost world around us.

Our themes are inter-linked. We are not going to out-preach the world unless we have out-thought the world. Nor are we going to out-preach the world if we do not preach in a spirit of love, so that the man of the world is overpowered by a 'double whammy'—by the gospel, which is the power of God for salvation, and by love.

What accounted for the success of the early church? It won the day in the realm of love. That is the third challenge facing us in present-day Britain.

4
The realm
of suffering

We have been considering what we ought to do if we would win our land back from the paganism of the present day. We have seen that there is a need to pray that God would move by his Holy Spirit in our day. But at the same time we have reminded ourselves of our responsibility in this area. We have seen that we are to win the day by out-thinking, out-preaching and out-loving this world.

But we can be sure that if we set about winning the day in the realm of the mind, in the realm of preaching, and by demonstrating love both within the church and to our neighbours outside the church, there will be a price to pay. As believers we must be ready to suffer.

Now we need to be perfectly clear about what kind of sufferings we mean. There is, as we know, suffering that is common to every member of the human race: failure, disappointment, frustration, sickness, ill health, bereavement, death—the whole range of difficult providences that people are confronted with, whether or not they are Christians. But what we are considering are those sufferings that come to us as a direct consequence of our being Christians.

Suffering as Christians

There are two categories of suffering that come across the paths of Christians just because they are Christians.

First of all, there is the suffering which arises from deliberate and conscious self-sacrifice, when the Christian is prepared to live without some of the comforts of life for the sake of the gospel. It is the suffering which arises from realising that as Christians we are in a battle, and if we seriously wish to fight, there is a price to pay.

Self-sacrifice

In his book *Evangelicalism in Britain 1935–1995*, Oliver Barclay, for many years General Secretary of the Inter-Varsity Fellowship (later called the UCCF), says of the Christians of the 1930s that they 'had a knowledge of the Bible that surpasses ours in the 1990s'. And he then goes on to say:

> They also had a willingness to apply what they found, if need be with a level of self-sacrifice that puts us to shame in our much more comfortable generation that will not risk careers, financial security or comfort . . . They knew that they were in a battle for the gospel.

The concept of a self-sacrificing Christianity is rare, if not unknown, today. Perhaps we still consider that venturing to the foreign mission field involves a degree of self-sacrifice, but even in this context things have changed. To quote Barclay again:

> The 1990s generation is not inclined to be committed to anything long-term . . . thus short-term Christian service is popular . . . to be committed to long-term missionary work or Christian ministry (for instance) is less compelling.

That is a perfectly fair description of our generation, is it not?

There is a version of the evangelical faith, a version that is found particularly in the USA, which maintains that when we become Christians all our difficulties will be solved. Becoming a Christian, it claims, is a panacea for all our ills, and henceforth life will be free of problems and suffering. Indeed, we shall be not only happier but richer because we are Christians. Small wonder that this 'health, wealth and prosperity gospel' is so popular!

But what a strange gospel this is! In the first place, nowhere does Scripture promise that we shall be spared the difficult providences of this world; and in the second place, how do we reconcile this with the self-sacrificing Christianity of the Bible? We have to ask ourselves: Does our Christianity cost us anything today? Do we suffer in any way for being Christian? Is there any self-sacrifice which causes us to suffer?

Paul, in his first epistle to the Corinthians, writes:

Do you not know that in a race all the runners run . . . ? Run in such a way as to get the prize. Everyone who competes in the games goes into strict training. They do it to get a crown that will not last; but we do it to get a crown that will last for ever. Therefore I do not run like a man running aimlessly; I do not fight like a man beating the air. No, I beat my body and make it my slave so that after I have preached to others, I myself will not be disqualified for the prize (9:24-27).

Self-discipline of necessity involves suffering. Does our personal devotion cost us anything? Does our service to the church cost us anything? Does our financial contribution to the church cost us anything? Do we know anything of what cost and self-sacrifice mean? Is there any effort, labour or sweat in our Christianity?

Persecution
The second kind of suffering that the Christian has to face is that which arises from persecution. Paul tells Timothy, 'Everyone

who wants to live a godly life in Christ Jesus will be persecuted' (2 Timothy 3:12). Because of our faith in the Lord Jesus Christ we are hated by the world in general, and that hatred manifests itself in scorn, physical persecution, imprisonment, torture, and even martyrdom. We do not go looking for persecution, but we should not be surprised if we have to face it. In Britain today there are signs that perhaps such persecution is coming.

If we want to win this land for Christ, we are never going to do so from our easy chairs, nor from the comfort of the saints' fellowship. There is a price to pay. And we have to be prepared to pay that price before we even contemplate winning the day in the realm of the mind, in the realm of preaching and declaring, and in the realm of love.

This is not going to be easy. We are living in a soft society, which seeks comfort and entertainment, and in which suffering of any kind is pushed to the periphery of human experience. There are all kinds of tablets available for the relief of pain, and all kinds of doctors ready to rid us of a variety of worries. In such an environment we have to face up to the possibility of having to suffer. In a day when everyone else is doing everything possible to avoid suffering, we have to take on the challenge that we are to out-suffer the world if we are to win the day.

Central to Christianity

As Christians we need to remind ourselves that suffering is central to Christianity. Without suffering there is no Christianity; were it not for the suffering of Christ there would not be a single Christian. Any version of Christianity which attempts to explain itself without even mentioning suffering, let alone putting it in the central position, is guilty of distorting the truth. Suffering is at the centre of God's plan of salvation.

From the beginning of the Bible to its end we are confronted with suffering. In the very first book, Genesis, when God comes into the garden after the Fall, he speaks to the serpent in these words: 'And I will put enmity between you and the woman, and between your offspring and hers; he will crush your head, and you will strike his heel' (Genesis 3:15). If there is to be salvation for mankind, suffering must come to the seed of the woman.

Again, in Isaiah 53 we read of the Suffering Servant. 'He . . . was led like a lamb to the slaughter, and as a sheep before her shearers is silent, so he did not open his mouth' (verse 7) 'He was pierced for our transgressions, he was crushed for our iniquities; the punishment that brought us peace was upon him, and by his wounds we are healed' (verse 5). What suffering!

The Gospel records

When we read the historical account of the life of the Lord Jesus Christ in the New Testament's four Gospels, we can look at his life as one of protracted suffering, culminating in the excruciating suffering on Calvary.

From heaven to earth

It could be said that there was suffering for Jesus in the very act of coming from heaven. We are told in Philippians, '[He] made himself nothing . . . he humbled himself' (Philippians 2:7-8). If you make yourself of no reputation, if you humble yourself, you suffer. We are sometimes forced to 'eat humble pie', and that is neither pleasant nor comfortable. There is a price to pay.

How much greater was the price paid by Christ when he humbled himself to come down to earth and take human flesh! The Omnipotent humbling himself into a tiny baby's weak body; the Omnipresent humbling himself to be confined to a mean corner of the earth for one moment of time; the Omniscient humbling himself to accept the mind and understanding of a child, and having to learn how to speak and how to read! It must have been at great cost to the Son of God.

But, more than that, Christ came down from a world of perfection to a sinful earth. If you are from a Christian home and background, you know what it is like to work with or to meet worldly people. The language is often coarse, the jokes tasteless, the talk empty and suggestive. It gets you down, and you long for five o'clock when you can return to your Christian family.

But your slight suffering bears no comparison with that of the Son of God. What he had in eternity was perfect companionship and fellowship with his Father and the Holy Spirit; and he had to leave that Paradise to come down to earth to befriend sinners, to live amongst difficult people, envious people, cruel people. How he must have suffered when he took the semblance of sinful man!

Jonathan Edwards, in one of his books, maintains that Jesus Christ suffered in the body even before he was born—in other words, he suffered in the womb. We know that doctors are of the opinion that what happens to the mother during pregnancy affects the unborn child. What happened to Mary during the days immediately prior to giving birth to Jesus? She had to undertake a long and uncomfortable journey from Nazareth to Bethlehem, a journey which must have had a harmful effect on her baby.

But there is more. Before the child was two years old, his parents had to cross the Gaza Strip and the Sinai Desert to escape the wrath of Herod. How would we have liked to take a child of that tender age on such a journey, whether on foot or on the back of an ass or a camel? The stifling heat of the day and the intense cold of the night, the thirst and the hunger, must have meant a great deal of suffering for Joseph, Mary and the little one. The child Jesus was suffering before he was old enough to understand.

Then, as Christ grew, he suffered famine and thirst. He knew what it was to be without a home. He knew what it was to be sad at the loss of loved ones.

Rejected and opposed

But there is more. He came to his Father's chosen people, the people his Father had showered abundantly with blessings: 'He came to that which was his own'—and what happened?—'but his own did not receive him' (John 1:11). Ostracism! Rejection! Persecution! There is nothing more unpleasant than having your family turn their backs on you, but that was Christ's experience. The chosen people of God did not want the Son of God. Yes, Christ suffered.

But there is still more. Jesus Christ was led to the wilderness for forty days to be tempted by Satan, to suffer the all-out attack of the Evil One. Although we are told that Satan then departed from him 'until an opportune time', he never gave up tempting him over the three years of his public ministry. The powers of darkness were always warring against him. Indeed, on one occasion he had to turn on Peter, one of his dearest disciples, and say, 'Get behind me, Satan!' (Matthew 16:23). Then there was the betrayal of Judas, one of the twelve. How that must have hurt!

Knowing what lay ahead

Yet there is more. He had to live his life knowing the death that lay ahead of him. Are you as thankful as I am that we do not know when or how we shall die? We could never live with such knowledge—it would be like a cloud over our lives. But he, at the age of twelve, could say, 'I had to be in my Father's house' (Luke 2:49). He knew what lay ahead. He explains matters to the disciples; he tells them that he must go up to Jerusalem to be condemned by the Pharisees and the authorities, and be put to death.

Jesus Christ knew that he would be murdered, and he had to live with that knowledge. Inevitably there would be suffering, and by the time he came to the Garden of Gethsemane he was conscious that the greatest suffering was at hand. He prays,

'Father, if you are willing, take this cup from me' (Luke 22:42). It was the cup of God's wrath. Small wonder that his sweat was like drops of blood!

Crucified and forsaken

There is yet more. The betrayal, the denial, the summary trial, the spitting, the mocking, the crown of thorns, the heavy cross, the nails, the hanging, the thirst, the jeering: 'Come down from the cross, if you are the Son of God' (Matthew 27:40). Forsaken by all his friends. Alone. There is nothing worse than suffering alone. Having someone to whisper a word of comfort in your ear is a help. But as Jesus hung on that cross there was no one to share his agony. Earth did not want him. He suffered alone on the cross.

But the worst is still to come. 'My God, my God, why have you forsaken me?' (Mark 15:34). Not only does earth not want him, but neither does heaven. That was the ultimate loneliness. Why did heaven not want him? Scripture provides the answer: 'He himself bore our sins in his body on the tree' (1 Peter 2:24). There is no room for sin in heaven. But more, the sword of God smote him at Calvary; the wrath of God was revealed from heaven against his Son as he bore our sins in his own body. At that agonising time he looks earthward and sees that all have fled, and then in the midst of his agony he looks heavenward and knows that the Father has forsaken him. That was the pinnacle of his suffering.

Suffering is central to Christianity. It is no accident that the symbol of Christianity down the ages has been a cross. Were it not for that suffering, we Christians would not be here.

'To this you were called'

In his first epistle Peter tells the scattered believers: 'To this you were called, because Christ suffered for you, leaving you an example, that you should follow in his steps' (1 Peter 2:21). Paul writes to the Romans in the same vein: 'Now if we are children, then we are heirs—heirs of God and co-heirs with Christ, if indeed we share in his sufferings in order that we may also share in his glory' (Romans 8:17). Again, in a personal letter to Timothy, Paul exhorts the young man, 'Endure hardship with us like a good soldier of Christ Jesus' (2 Timothy 2:3).

Jesus himself at the very beginning of his ministry, in what we call the Sermon on the Mount, had warned his disciples of the inevitability of suffering: 'Blessed are those who are persecuted . . . Blessed are you when people insult you, persecute you and falsely say all kinds of evil against you because of me' (Matthew 5:10-11). And Christ's disciples down the ages have suffered such treatment. We are expected to share his suffering. We have to be prepared do so. That is what our faith is about.

Fellow soldiers

When Christ was dying on the cross, his suffering was twofold. In the first place there was the suffering he endured in his unique propitiatory role—he took the penalty for our sin in his own body. That is something only he could do. But there was also the suffering which emanated from the battle against Satan and the forces of darkness, and it is this role we are expected to share with him. As we become united with Christ, members of his body, we become fellow soldiers in the constant war against evil.

The suffering can sometimes lead to death. In 1 John 3:16 we read, 'This is how we know what love is: Jesus Christ laid down his life for us. And we ought to lay down our lives for our brothers.' When out-loving reaches its pinnacle, it moves to the realm of suffering, even martyrdom, for the brethren.

That is what happened in the case of the apostles. Peter and John were thrown into prison because they were 'teaching the people and proclaiming in Jesus the resurrection of the dead'

(Acts 4:2). The academic Paul, who forfeited a comfortable life in order to follow the Saviour who arrested him on the Damascus road, suffered all manner of tribulations on his missionary journeys. Writing to Timothy to warn him of perilous times ahead, he reminds him of the persecutions and afflictions he endured in Antioch, Iconium and Lystra, adding, 'In fact, everyone who wants to live a godly life in Christ Jesus will be persecuted' (2 Timothy 3:12). Warfare means confronting the enemy, and being prepared to pay the ultimate price if necessary. This Stephen did when the church was in its infancy, as did James, the brother of John, soon afterwards.

A word of warning

Having received forgiveness of sins and the hope of everlasting life, Christians are summoned to battle, and the inevitable consequence of this is that they will suffer by way of self-sacrifice and persecution. But a word of warning lest anyone think that this suffering comes in an intentional way.

It is not that we say, 'I'll go home to sacrifice myself, to be persecuted.' Rather, suffering is something that arises as a consequence of a desire to serve God. We put our effort into out-thinking, out-preaching and out-loving, and as we do these things we find there is a cost—suffering.

For instance, when trying to win the day in the realm of the mind, we might have to be prepared to sweat in order to master theological books, or sacrifice a leisurely summer weekend to attend a theological course. If we are ready to give time to witnessing and proclaiming the Word, there will be a cost to pay. And if we are going to love our neighbour and fellow Christian as we ought, it will cost us.

It is as we pursue the service of God that the suffering comes. Therefore, if we are serious about winning the day in the realm of the mind, the realm of preaching and the realm of love, we must consider the possibility of having to sacrifice something. God will come to you and say, 'This is what I want you to do, and this is what it will cost.'

Consolations

'Who is sufficient for these things?' you might ask. What consolation is there for us as we respond to this call? There are two consolations held out in the Scriptures.

Paul tells the Corinthians: 'For just as the sufferings of Christ flow over into our lives, so also through Christ our comfort overflows' (2 Corinthians 1:5). The more you know of self-sacrifice and persecution, the more you will know of the consolations that abound. You will not lose out. Sometimes we know little of the comfort because we have known nothing of the suffering.

He will be with us

God loves his children, and he knows beforehand that they will suffer if they are zealous for his kingdom. 'Blessed are you when people insult you, persecute you and falsely say all kinds of evil against you'—for you will be recompensed for every suffering. Jesus Christ does not ask any one of his followers to endure more than he himself suffered. In the hour of self-denial and persecution, Christ will be with us (Matthew 28:20). And he will repay us a hundredfold.

We shall be with him

There is also another consolation. How did Jesus Christ endure his suffering? How was he able to face the persecution, the agony and the death? We find the answer in Hebrews 12:

> Therefore . . . let us throw off everything that hinders and the sin that so easily entangles, and let us run with perseverance the race marked out for us. Let us fix our eyes on Jesus, the

author and perfecter of our faith, who for the joy set before him endured the cross, scorning its shame, and sat down at the right hand of the throne of God (verses 1-2).

We might think that because Jesus was the Son of God and perfect man he could cope with all the sufferings that came to him without the need of encouragement. Not so! He received encouragement by fixing his gaze on 'the joy set before him'. It was this that enabled him to endure the cross. As he rode into Jerusalem on the donkey he was looking upward. As Judas betrayed him, his sights were beyond the betrayal. As the courts falsely judged him, his eyes were fixed on the reward. As he carried the cross, he foresaw the unspeakable joy of heaven and of eternity. 'After the suffering of his soul, he will see the light of life and be satisfied' (Isaiah 53:11). That is how Jesus Christ had the strength to go on.

Is that not what can be said of all the saints down the ages? We read of Moses:

He chose to be ill-treated along with the people of God rather than to enjoy the pleasures of sin for a short time. He regarded disgrace for the sake of Christ as of greater value than the treasures of Egypt, because he was looking ahead to his reward (Hebrews 11:25-26).

He looked upward, and was ready to suffer affliction with the people of God. Again, the writer tells the Hebrews, 'You sympathised with those in prison and joyfully accepted the confiscation of your property, because you knew that you yourselves had better and lasting possessions' (10:34). How could the saints of the early church bear losing their possessions in persecution? Because they had treasure laid up in heaven, 'where moth and rust do not destroy, and where thieves do not break in and steal' (Matthew 6:20).

Remember the words of Romans 8:17. 'Now if we are children, then we are heirs—heirs of God and co-heirs with Christ, if indeed we share in his sufferings in order that we may also share in his glory.' Note the verse that follows: 'I consider that our present sufferings are not worth comparing with the glory that will be revealed in us.' Then again, writing to the Corinthians, Paul encourages his readers with these words:

Therefore we do not lose heart. Though outwardly we are wasting away, yet inwardly we are being renewed day by day. For our light and momentary troubles are achieving for us an eternal glory that far outweighs them all. *So we fix our eyes not on what is seen, but on what is unseen. For what is seen is temporary, but what is unseen is eternal* (2 Corinthians 4:16-18).

Let us close with the words of Christ in the Sermon on the Mount:

Blessed are you when people insult you, persecute you and falsely say all kinds of evil against you because of me. Rejoice and be glad, because great is your reward in heaven, for in the same way they persecuted the prophets who were before you (Matthew 5:11-12).

If suffering comes our way, we have these consolations. He is with us, and one day we shall be with him in heaven, beyond the reach of all suffering. That eternal hope is our motivation to self-sacrifice and facing persecution in this world.

The challenge

A great work faces the church in Britain in the years ahead. Our desire is to see the tide of paganism reversed, to see this idolatrous, immoral and multi-faith land of ours turn to Christ.

The church in the early centuries was faced with a similar situation. The first Christians took the gospel into the world of their day and, under the influence of the Holy Spirit, they were victorious. They out-thought, they out-preached, they out-loved, and they won the day because they were ready to suffer in order to accomplish those things. Let us go and do likewise.